GARDENS OF MY LIFE

Dixie Shoopman

Gardens of My Life

©2021 Dixie Shoopman

print ISBN: 978-1-66780-423-1
ebook ISBN: 978-1-66780-424-8

CONTENTS

PREFACE

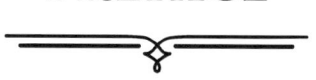

Awhile back, when I was listening to Mom tell some visitor about one of her gardens, I realized that I was hearing some details I'd never heard before. I knew about how many hours she spent with Nene in the violet bed, and I remembered washing off carrots with the garden hose and eating them warm from the ground. I was there when she learned about Findhorn, and I watched her herbs grow.

I'm sure my siblings and I could compile our memories, as our lives overlapped around our mother's gardens. But we only know our experiences, not hers. And when I listen to her telling other people about those gardens, I often hear details that I never pictured before.

Later, I told her that if she ever wondered what to give me for my birthday or Christmas, I could give her an idea right now.

"What?"

"I wish you'd write down everything you can remember about your favorite gardens."

"My favorite gardens?"

"Yes."

"But you already know all about them."

Nevertheless, she did write them down, and I'm sharing my mother's gift with you.

-Gretchen Bernabei

MY DAD'S GARDENS

My dad had two gardens I remember. The first was located behind our house on Texas Avenue, the little house I was born in. My memories of that house are pretty spotty, as I was still young when we moved to East Pearce, where we lived the rest of my life at home.

Dad's garden I remember is part of my earliest recollections, and it is mainly just a series of mental pictures:

There was a peach tree at one side of the vegetable garden, and when it bloomed, the pink blossoms were my very first sight of springtime beauty. Though I was very young, probably no more than four years old, the sight of that peach tree still floats up in my memory bank from time to time.

One day my dad was digging potatoes when he stopped suddenly and came walking to me where I knelt beside a row of young lettuce plants.

"Look what I found, Jody; a tiny baby potato!"

He handed me a little Irish potato, perfectly formed, exactly like its parents, no bigger than my father's thumb. Well I was completely enchanted with that tiny potato and carried it around with me for several days.

The peach tree and the baby potato are the only two absolutely clear memories I have of that early garden. However, I do have a very comfortable, nurtured feeling when I think of spending time among the lettuce and carrots and onions and potatoes, watching my dad and listening to him as he worked in the soil.

EAST PEARCE GARDEN

In 1939 my folks had our Texas Avenue house moved to several lots behind our current home. They had it completely remodeled, and we enjoyed a much bigger house and yard after the move.

There was a nice-sized garden spot behind the garage, and my dad maintained a wonderful garden back there. He grew nothing but vegetables, and I helped him a little bit with weeding, planting, and harvesting.

There was nothing really spectacular or memorable about that garden. It was pretty ordinary. Dad grew all the usual seasonal vegetables, tomatoes, peppers, green beans, onions, squash, okra, garlic, potatoes, all in spring and summer. In fall we had tomatoes and the winter crop: turnip greens, collards, mustard greens, carrots, sweet potatoes (planted in summer, harvested in fall), beets, anything that liked cooler weather. Dad always planted four or five rows of cabbage. He liked to make homemade sauerkraut.

One of my favorite memories of that garden has to do with his cabbage plants.

I liked to go out into the garden in the late afternoon. I had come home from school, done homework, ridden my bike or played games with neighbor kids, and returned home hot and sweaty, almost but not quite time for supper.

I liked to go out in the garden behind the garage, lie down in the cabbage row, and drink the dew which had collected in big leaves of cabbage. There was a trick to it. You had to lie on your side, tilt your head, tip one leaf carefully, until the few drops of water rolled into your mouth. There wasn't much water but it was heavenly delicious, always cool and faintly cabbagy tasting. I went from plant to plant until I had gotten a pretty good drink.

Later in life I have thought many times about that quirky little activity. It still seems like a good way to get a drink of water.

GRANNY PUMPHREY'S VEGETABLE GARDEN

I started spending time in Edna, at Granny and Pa's house, so early in life that I remember being carried in from the car riding on Sissie's hip. I spent huge chunks of my childhood and adolescence there. My Edna experience takes in six or seven eras of my life as well as six or seven areas of that magical place.

One of the important areas of my days is centered in Granny's garden. Granny worked in her garden every single morning, rain or shine. She didn't always spend the whole morning out there, but the plants were inspected and tended-to each day in whichever way was needed: watering, weeding, picking, even killing a rattlesnake or two. Granny had help, too, and that to me, seems almost miraculous. Newt, the black man, was there to help in the yard, the garden, and "around the place." He came, along with Ferlie for inside the house, six days a week.

Granny's garden was big. I don't know if it was a whole acre or more than that, but I know that she grew several long rows of strawberries, along with enough room for watermelons, cantaloupes, cucumbers, squash, Irish potatoes and sweet potatoes, and about ten rows of corn. And those are just the crops that require lots of room. Also the squash family had to be separated from each other in order to avoid cross-pollinating. So those vining, creeping plants like yams and squash needed lots of room.

In addition to all the room-taking plants, Granny consistently planted several types of tomatoes, okra, bell peppers, butter beans, crowder peas, and green beans.

One of my favorite things to do in her garden involved the strawberry rows. I was never told to leave the berries alone. There were so many strawberries that I was permitted, whenever I felt like it, to sit down among the plants and eat all I could hold. Of course, I sat out there very often, scooting along on my rear, picking and gorging on the biggest and reddest berries I could find.

I was no help to Granny in the garden. I never pulled a weed or cultivated around a plant. Never held a hoe or a sharpshooter. I just visited with Granny and Newt as they worked, and I picked and ate some of everything growing out there.

Now I did help pick a few vegetables from time to time, beans and peas especially. But as I picked, I had company: Granny, Newt and Sissie helped pick sometimes when the beans were in desperate need of being harvested. But mainly, I just watched and asked questions and listened to the grownups as they worked.

When the crops came in during the summer, we all gathered on the front porch and "worked them up." We snapped beans, shelled peas, skinned tomatoes, prepared all those vegetables for either cooking for dinner or for canning for the winter. Of all the vegetables we dealt with on the porch, my favorite was the butter bean.

The butter bean was nice to work with for several reasons: It was clean. No runny juice or sticky stems to make hands and arms miserable. Also, each bean was different. They did have the same shapes, but the coloring and patterning were wildly dissimilar. Nene would say that some of them were "downright gaudy." The beans had a background white or cream shade, but the splashes of color were in pink, magenta, even dark purple, and they looked almost exactly like some of the very modern paintings I've seen in museums, the paintings where the artist has thrown paint at the canvas. Just splashes and splotches. Sometimes I would open a butter bean and think I saw the shape of an animal or a face. I never saw the shape of Jesus or the Virgin Mary, but once I made Sissie laugh hard when I showed her a butter bean and asked if she didn't see the exact shape of Aunt Clay's nose. Yes, butter beans were fun to "work up."

Tomatoes, not so much. When the tomatoes "came in," we marshaled all the family, aunts, cousins, nears and dears, and gathered on the front porch for hours for several days. The tomatoes were brought in from the garden to the back porch. Newt brought them in big buckets and dishpans, carrying one bucket and pulling a red wagon with a couple of buckets on it. At the back porch, Ferlie washed the tomatoes, then took them into the kitchen where they were poured into huge pots of boiling water. After being scalded for only a couple of minutes, they were dipped out and put back into the now-washed buckets and dishpans. Next, they were carried to the front porch where five or six people waited with buckets and pots and pans and dishpans. I was always one of the "skinners" on the porch with a paring knife.

On the porch, we picked up each tomato, slicked off the skin, and put all the peeled tomatoes together. When we had gone through those tomatoes, the next batch would arrive from the kitchen.

It seemed to me that the tomato chain never ended. We absolutely drowned in tomatoes. And then, at some point, Granny would stop the assembly, and she and Ferlie would go to the kitchen and start "putting up" the day's batch. I think she canned maybe eight or nine dozen cans of tomatoes each day we worked them up. I do know that there were five or six shelves of canned tomatoes in the pantry by the time we left tomatoes and moved on the butter beans or green beans or whatever came in next.

I just remembered something else about these front porch sessions. During our afternoons, we listened to the radio. From about noon until four or 4:30, we heard soap operas like "Pepper Young's Family" and "Lorenzo Jones and his devoted wife Belle," and everyone's favorite, "Guiding Light." There were several others I can't remember, but our afternoons were full of drama. Granny, Sissie, Nene, Aunt Clay, and several others each had comments and judgments about some of the characters and situations from those soaps. They consistently predicted that Lorenzo's daughter ought to be careful dating that Bill character. He sounded like a shady sort who was up to no good. They also worried about Bert Bauer's husband because he seemed to be drinking a little too much.

The soaps filled our afternoons, along with the tomatoes and okra, green beans and squash.

We didn't deal with vegetables only. Putting up fruits took a deal of time also. Strawberries came in early, even before the vegetables. We washed and hulled basketsful of strawberries every day for several weeks. Each morning they were picked, washed, hulled, and sent to the kitchen.

Granny kept three or four pans of strawberry preserves going simultaneously during those days. She didn't use any Cert or Sure-Jell. The preserves were strawberries and sugar, cooked down slowly until they were thick and spreadable. The whole house smelled like strawberries when the preserves were being made. Granny's preserves were bright red. No food coloring. She said they retained their color because they were so slowly cooked. She provided strawberry preserves for all the families, Aunt Ray, Bud, Dordu, us as well as jars and jars for Aunt Clay, Frances, Gina Lee, Uncle Travis's family, Katherine

Simons's family, and several other cousins too numerous to mention. And the strawberries didn't all go into the preserve pots. We ate shortcake and strawberry parfait and strawberry pies galore.

My favorite way, besides in the field, was chopped up, sugared, and mashed into a mound of home-made cottage cheese (the family called it "curd") and drowned in a sea of heavy cream. Really good!

Around the same time, depending on the winter, the dewberries got ripe. We had a fence across the front of the garden, and it was covered with dewberry vines. We didn't harvest nearly as many dewberries as strawberries, of course, but a few cobblers showed up during dewberry season, and Granny put up a good many jars of dewberry jelly.

I remember one particular experience by the dewberry fence one day. I think I was about seven or eight, standing with my coffee can, picking the shiny back dewberries when I felt like someone was watching me. I don't know, really, what it felt like, only I became aware that I should look closely at the berries, some kind of sixth sense. I began to focus on the berry vines in front of me, and realized that I was almost nose to nose with an enormous copperhead lying on the fence rail, sunning himself. We looked at each other eye to eye, and I took tiny Tim Conway steps back and back, out of his reach, then turned and ran for Granny. She brought her hoe, but the snake slithered away before she could whack him. After that little experience I made sure to sing or rattle around as I approached the dewberry patch, just to make sure I scared any snakes away.

I'm not sure just when the figs got ripe, but when they did mature, we harvested every single one. Granny and Pa had two old, big fig trees and about 4 smaller ones. They produced what my folks called "blue figs." They were rather small, very dark in color, and sweet as sugar. These days lots of people here in Texas raise hybrid figs that are huge: very pretty, but not much taste (sort of like California fruit, as told by 4-finger Woo).

We ate a lot of figs fresh with heavy cream, but most of them were made into fig preserves. Our fig preserves were made with unpeeled fruit. All we did was wash them, then Granny would cook them down, whole, with a tiny bit of stem left on. She simmered them with some sugar and sliced up lemons. Then they were jarred and sealed. By the time they were fully cooked, most of them had broken up, but there were still lots of whole figs in the jar. They were sort of hard to eat with biscuits or toast, because of the really big lumps. They were hard to spread, but they were really, really good.

I bought some fig preserves at the annual Methodist Women's Garage Sale in Dripping Springs a few years ago, and discovered that the figs were mashed up. The preserves were very tasty, but I sort of missed finding the whole fruit in there. It made me wonder if cooking the whole fig was just our family way of making the preserves, or if it was a

Southern way. Whichever, fig preserves took up another segment of our summer canning routine.

Pears got ripe in late summer or early fall. Again, we gathered on the porch and peeled pears while Lorenzo Jones and his devoted wife, Belle sought the American Dream, simultaneously selling Ivory Snow.

Pear time was easy. There wasn't a flood of the fruit, just enough to keep us busy for a few days. The pears were peeled and sliced for two main things: pear preserves and pear relish. The preserves were similar to all other jellies, jams, and preserves, mostly just cooked down with sugar and some spices. However, the relish Granny made with pears was the absolute best, ever.

Several years ago a neighbor gave me a bag of pears and I dug out Granny's old recipe. I had never made pear relish, and I had no idea whether mine would be edible or not. I didn't grind the pears like Granny and my mother had done years ago. I put mine through the new-fangled food processor and they looked exactly the same as they did back in the day. I mixed up the ingredients, followed the cooking/canning procedures and ended up with a few jars of old-timey, authentic, absolutely heavenly pear relish.

It is still the best. It's good on pinto beans and burgers. It's good mixed into deviled eggs, but there is nothing in this world that can redeem a plain old nasty wiener like that pear relish spread thick on a hot dog. Makes me drool just thinking about it.

And it's funny. I had, once again, a Marcel Proust memory moment the first time I tasted my own pear relish as an adult. Suddenly it all came back: summertime, very hot weather at Granny's house, and sights and sounds and smells of those lazy days flooding me through and through.

It's funny, though. I just wrote "lazy days," and they were anything but lazy. And yet, there was never, at least to me, a sense of rush, urgency or stress of any kind from any of those folks. Slow pace, simple life. What a gift to my childhood.

NENE'S FLOWER GARDEN

The seasons of my life have been accentuated by gardens of one kind or another. Some of them overlapped, but each one, in its own way, fills the vault of my memories.

During the same years of my dad's and Granny's gardens, I spent great chunks of time in Nene's flower garden. I wish I were an artist or even a decent draftsman because I would like to show a layout of Nene's garden.

Located on the west side of Granny's house, the garden itself was the entire length of the structure, plus about 20 or 30 feet past the back door. It was bordered by the house on the left and the garage on the back. The entire right side was open to a dirt driveway. Across the driveway was a wide open pasture, leading to a creek about a quarter-mile down.

If you walked up to Nene's garden from the front, you would see an arbor for the entrance. Several things covered the arbor. Nene seemed to trade them out from time to time: roses, wisteria, yellow jasmine. Several different looks down the years.

Inside the arbor were stepping stones set in rows and circles, each segment designed for a specific flower. These stones were simply concrete ovals, not real stones at all, but they made perfect walkways, and they made paths and individual beds throughout the garden. Consequently, Nene was able to keep beds of something blooming almost all year long.

During those years of growing up with Nene in her flower garden, I was able to pick up, just as naturally as breathing, the habits and preferences of quite a few common flowers and ferns and shrubs. There were no big box stores at that time. No one sold flower plants, not even the feed store. So we planted almost everything by seeds, then watched them sprout and send up their tiny leaves. It was a patient, slow process, and I learned to identify dozens of seedlings from their tiniest appearance. I still really love watching seeds come up and present their very own identity. Each one is its own little self.

As we planted seeds and talked about them and watched them grow and bloom, Nene and I also dug new beds, watered plants, pulled weeds, did the myriad of maintenance chores that have to happen in a really well-loved garden.

And during a great deal of that maintenance work, Nene and I talked and talked and talked. She pointed out how some seeds, like the nasturtium, are large and hard. They like to be soaked overnight so they have an easy time sprouting. Some seeds, like the larkspur, are so tiny that's it's good to plant them with a handful of sand or even corn meal, to keep them well spaced, not too crowded. My gardening lessons came about so slowly and so naturally that I never had a clue that I was learning anything. Water and mulch and humus were just part and parcel of the process.

As we squatted together, pulling nut grass and cultivating the alyssum or zinnias or candytuft, Nene not only commented on plants, but she also told me stories. I heard all about King Arthur, Lancelot, Sir Gawain, and their adventures, and Nene gave Robin Hood a good go also.

I was in college when I recognized the stories of several Shakespearean plays. They had been relayed to me with a backdrop of phlox and pansies and sweet peas. Every now and then Nene would say she had run dry of stories. When I insisted that she could make one up, she did, and we sat there, scratching in the dirt, while Nene spun me stories about me and all the wonderful adventures I had when I lived in England or in the jungle, or in ancient Greece. Her original Dixie stories, of course, were my favorites.

Today I look back on that flower garden with great fondness. So many lessons were learned there: patience and horticulture and language. However, the overriding layer of the lessons was the awareness and the memory of great beauty.

MAPLETON

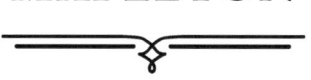

The Mapleton chapter of my life is ten years long. We moved to our little house with an acre of yard in 1957 and moved into our big dream house in 1967. During those ten Mapleton years, our girls grew from pre-school to pre-teens; Hank was born and moved on up to second grade by 1967. We went through a destructive hurricane, rebuilt from it, and had the predictably mundane milestones one would expect from ordinary middle-class folks. Ups and downs, but mostly satisfying and positive.

During the years, I rediscovered the soul-deep pleasure of gardening. After the hurricane, when Bert was re-building our house, the children and I spent most of our time outdoors. Bert managed to find time from his carpentry/repair work in the house to dig me a large, kidney-shaped flower bed in our back yard. The soil was very good without much help, so I had no trouble getting a beautiful array of annuals to grow and bloom. We had a big adventure moving a washed-up tree stump, dragged into the back yard from down the street. Placed at one end of the flower bed, it was my big dream to have a waterfall splashing down it with maidenhair fern growing out of a couple of its crevices. That dream never came true, but we all enjoyed the enormous tree stump in the flowerbed. The children climbed all over it regularly, and I did have small plants blooming in and around it from time to time.

The real garden of Mapleton, though, was my vegetable garden located in front and on the west side of the house.

When Bert got the house livable after the storm, and we had been settled for a few months, I asked if we couldn't dig up a nice-sized garden for vegetables, since the back flower bed was always chock full of flowers with no room for even one radish in it.

Bert borrowed his dad's tiller and went to work, digging into the lush St. Augustine lawn, thick as a carpet. We shook out all the grass, did the work of preparing the soil, and finally were ready to plant the garden.

This was my first honest-to-goodness garden to actively plan and plant. I had watched my dad, Granny Pumphrey, and numerous relatives and friends as they maintained their vegetable gardens, but I really didn't know a lot about exactly when and where to put specific plants.

It turned out that I knew more than I realized, and the Mapleton Garden was a sure-enough success. It was beautiful, and it was bountiful.

I planted it seasonally, as my folks had done. We had cabbage and greens, turnips, mustard, collard, as well as spinach and several lettuces, beets and carrots in the fall and winter. Then in spring and summer there were the usual heat-lovers: peppers, tomatoes of about six varieties, okra, and green beans.

We ate very well out of my garden, and the neighbors and kin got a good many bags of our produce. The children had fun picking tomatoes — big ones and Tiny Tims, loading them into their red wagon and going to neighbors, selling them to our friends. The neighbors consistently bought a few from the kids, even though most of them grew tomatoes in their own backyards.

I love hearing Gretchen tell about going out to the garden, squatting down, and pulling up a long, beautiful carrot, then wiping off the dirt with her hands, eating it like a little rabbit, right there in Mr. McGregor's garden.

During those years Bert's parents did a lot of shrimping in Trinity Bay nearby. They saved the shrimp heads for us, and Bert and I buried them in my garden in between crops. Consequently, the already nice soil became even better: fertilized and humus-filled. The garden really flourished.

One day Bert's dad drove up and joined me as I was working in the garden. It was a very early spring morning and I was getting ready to start on some early planting. He had a bag of something with him and asked if he could have one row of my garden. I said, "Sure." And he opened up his bag to show me a big bunch of bulbs. He had brought about 50 gladiola bulbs! I had never planted flowers in the garden, though I had seen zinnia and cosmos in some people's rows. I had never heard of companion planting at that time, though many old timers knew about it. Anyway, these glads that Papa brought were not for any particular horticultural benefit at all. He just liked gladiolas and didn't have a place to plant them at their house.

I was happy to have them, and he and I got a row ready and planted them that very morning. Later that year, in the summertime, those glads were absolutely spectacular. I have grown glads since then, but never have they been as tall and straight, as deeply vibrant and gorgeous as those glads in the Mapleton garden: red and pinks, whites, lavender and gold!

The Mapleton garden occupied me and has been a significant memory to our children.

The most dramatic and episodic garden event, however, had to do with a birthday gift I got from my mother.

That particular year, instead of the usual piece of clothing, G.W. gave me money for my birthday. Twenty-five dollars was a substantial sum those days, and I was thrilled to have some money to spend any way in the world that I wanted. I gave considerable thought to what I would buy with the unexpected windfall. Mom had made only one condition with the gift. "Don't buy groceries or pay the light bill with this money. Spend it on yourself."

Well I enjoyed several days of deciding: new sandals? A purse? A new bathing suit? It was a pleasant little mental activity, dreaming about what to buy.

Before I could decide or go shopping, the solution to my fantasies came down the road in a dump truck. The children and I were in the yard; kids up in the sweet gum tree, me in the garden nearby – just a usual spring day, warm and bright. The dump truck stopped outside our fence. A man got out and I walked over to speak with him, thinking he needed directions to someplace or other. No, he said, he was selling fertilizer for gardens, and he could see I had a nice plot going. We talked a little about what was planted, what we needed from weather — the usual things we talk about with others who are sharing our plant-growing struggles and successes. There were two men together, and the second man got out of the truck and joined us at the fence. They told me the fertilizer they were selling was a combination of rice hulls and sheep manure – very wonderful stuff for providing both humus and nutrients in the soil.

I went out the gate, joined them at the back of the truck, and looked at all that fine mulch, heaped and mountained in the back of the truck. At that moment I had a serious attack of greed and lust and desire. I absolutely coveted that stuff for my garden.

The first man had already quoted me a price. I thought it was, or seemed to me too expensive and I wondered if I could afford a bucket or two of the stuff.

We talked about how good it was. I am sure that they saw how much I wanted it.

Both men came into the yard, and I gave them some iced tea while we walked around the garden, talking about which plants were where, just general plant talk with friends.

Finally, we got around to how much I could buy. By this time, both men were charmed by the children, and we had established that I was itching to get some of that fine rice mulch.

The first man finally said, "Heck, Ma'am. It's late in the day. You want this stuff. How much money would you be able to spend on the whole load?"

Without a flicker I said, "Twenty-five dollars. That's all I have."

"That'll be fine. Where do you want us to dump it?"

"You mean the whole thing?" I asked.

"Sure, why not?" he grinned.

And so the two men returned to the truck; we opened the gate and stood back while the drove across the yard, in front of the sweet gum tree. Twitching with excitement, I watched as they poured the entire dump truck load on the far side of the garden: a veritable mountain of treasure.

I ran in, got my money and paid the fellows who were grinning and chuckling like they were tickled to death. I was just dancing with joy!

I had found the best, the best of the best birthday present ever.

That marvelous mulch was like a small mountain in our yard, but only for a few days. We spread the stuff six inches deep over every bit of garden, nestling it around the few things I had growing at that time. I dug some in deep, left some on top, used wheelbarrow after wheelbarrow full on every flower bed and tree in the yard, gave a can or two to Mr. Kelley and Mr. Griggs, our neighbors, and still had a hillock of fine rich mulch at the foot of the garden.

And did the garden like it? My goodness yes! We got almost freakishly big, crazy, deep-colored vegetables after that birthday bonanza. I scattered a few larkspur seeds around the base of the left-over pile, and they were so spectacular that some of them were actually three-pronged — not double, but triple. I've never seen any others like them.

I have seen a vintage cartoon picture of Queen Victoria looking especially stiff-faced-mean, frowning, and disapproving, with the caption, "We are not amused." That cartoon picture of Her Majesty is a dead ringer for my mother's reaction to the way I spent her birthday money. No amount of telling her how much pleasure and pure joy I got from the experience and from the use of that mulch could change her mind or expression. I don't believe she ever really forgave me for spending her birthday money buying fertilizer.

Be that as it may, the mulch pile episode made my Mapleton Garden an especially happy memory in my crazy-quilt catalog of growing things.

I really did love that garden!

PAPA'S KENTUCKY VEGETABLE GARDEN

Bert's dad retired from Exxon when he was 55 years old and returned to the farm his family had owned since he was a child. During his Kentucky retirement years he grew 100 apple trees, black Angus cattle, and alfalfa fields to feed the cattle. He also maintained an enormous vegetable garden.

He was not an organic gardener, though he came close to being one. He really despised "newfangled ideas" that became popular during the 60's and 70's: New Age stuff. However, he did practice some old-fashioned but very good gardening rituals.

Each year he cleaned out the barn and spread all the manure on his garden. Then he tilled it under and let it sit for a while. Finally, he tilled again and got ready to plant. Although he never used any mulch, never companion planted, and never ran a water hose to the garden, he managed to raise and harvest prodigious amounts of vegetables.

The garden itself was 1/2 acre, and for the first few years (before Bert & I moved to the farm) the only two people who were dealing with all this food were Granny and Papa! Needless to say, they gave away bushels of beans and squash to neighbors, friends, and relatives. But they still had enormous overflows of produce every summer when the crops came in.

Since they were firm believers in frugality, they bought a new freezer every so often, filling it full. There were two freezers in the basement, one chest-type and one upright in the garage. Also one in the mud room, just inside the back door. I don't believe they ever, ever threw away any package of frozen vegetables, no matter how old, frostbitten and colorless they became.

Papa planted three or four long rows of cabbage. And he did use most of it. Though they didn't eat cooked cabbage, they did consume a good bit of sauerkraut, which Papa made and aged in big old crocks in the basement. And it was really delicious stuff. Homemade kraut is the best.

Besides the cabbage, Papa planted Kentucky Wonder green beans; that was the only variety he considered fit to eat. There were several other varieties that I liked, bush varieties that were slow to mature and crisp and round, but Papa wanted no part of them. So we harvested bushels and bushels of green beans, many of which were over-sized and tough and stringy as mule hide. But none were wasted.

Along with cabbage and beans, Papa grew one or two rows of broccoli. He said that was his new-fangled crop. They had never grown broccoli when he was young, and he considered it pretty exotic.

There were always about five or six rows of tomatoes, always Better Boy. No other type was grown. We also drowned in them when they came in. Granny canned hundreds of jars of tomatoes and made tomato juice out of others.

Besides the other vegetables, Papa grew Irish potatoes, enough to store for winter, and sweet corn. Lots of it.

Occasionally he would try to grow cantaloupe and watermelon, but without success. I don't know if it was because coons and possums got them before they could ripen, but we never had any melons from the garden.

We did have summer squash. Again, it was a heavy-yielder, so whenever company came, they had to leave with a big bag of squash.

After we moved to Kentucky, Papa agreed to plant one row of okra, at my request. We all liked it fried, but none of us much liked to pick it. It's sticky and sharp-edged and miserable to pick.

Papa grew the plants of his youth, and he used the same tools and practices that his mother and grandmother had used before him. Though they used a mule, Papa did graduate to a John Deere tiller and plow. However, he grew acres of weeds because he didn't mulch, so he used a hand-me-down hoe to cultivate.

In spite of all the hard-nosed habits, and in spite of a dozen attitudes I didn't agree with or appreciate, he did produce a lot of food for a bunch of people.

When we moved to Kentucky, I tried to talk to Papa about organic gardening practices, such as companion planting, trying a number of different vegetables, mulching. However Papa took a pass on all my suggestions and that was fine. He grew up eating meat, potatoes, sauerkraut, green beans, and stewed apples and pretty much nothing else. German German German.

I just remembered. Two different years he did plant a few spinach seeds and we had wilted spinach salad. Very tasty. But they never ever cooked spinach. They thought it was inedible.

Papa's garden gave me a several-year experience with a whole different approach to life. Parts of it were hard to take, but I learned some important lessons.

I learned patience enough to endure through disapproval. Papa thought I was new-fangled and not trustworthy in the garden. I learned how to use his ways with pretty much of a stiff upper lip and good cheer.

I also learned to dig potatoes and to tell when the corn is ready to pick. Lots of practical stuff like that.

And I learned, by just being so close to the soil again, the transformative spirituality of being among green things growing.

MY FINDHORN GARDEN

In 1974 when we moved to the Kentucky farm from Okinawa, I began a whole new phase in life. We all did.

I began reading garden books, checked out at the local library, and discovered a new world of plants and attitudes and experiments. I discovered herbs, but there were none available anywhere around Somerset, Kentucky. Not plants, not seeds. I just read about them.

I subscribed to *Organic Gardener* magazine and learned all about companion planting, drip irrigation, raised beds, mulching, and natural pest control.

Some of the things I read were pretty esoteric. One book dealt with the meditative gardening practices in the Himalayas. Not too practical for me, but wildly interesting. I read several books dealing with the secret life of plants, how Luther Burbank heard his cactus tell him to eliminate spines on prickly pear, thus rendering them suitable as feed for cattle and delicacies for people.

I can't say that I bought into every single thing I read, but I certainly did become a firm believer in the communication that takes place between people and their plants, if the people are open to it.

During the first couple of years, Bert built me a raised bed in the back yard, and I tried some new things. He built, or rather assembled, an old thrown out, rusted metal trough, and I used it as a seedbed. Through *Organic Gardening* I had found a place called Nichols Farms in Oregon that sold herb seeds, so I ordered a collection of the ones I had read about. They all came up, and I was on my way to an absorbing and enduring romance with growing and using herbs.

One thing led to another of course, and I met several people who were as interested and curious as I was about growing herbs of all kinds: aromatic, medicinal, culinary, decorative. Another world opened up for me, and I've never become tired of raising herbs. I just love a nice, compact little herb garden. I also just love a wild, mix-and-match helter-skelter herb garden where some of the little fellows have jumped their borders and run amuck in each other's spaces.

During the time I was learning about and planting herbal flowers, I read a book about the Findhorn garden in Scotland. Located on the coast, right on the North Sea, some people developed a garden, which, in spite of impossible soil and weather conditions, produced incredible, absolutely unbelievable crops.

I've forgotten the people's name, but there were several of them, and they used composting, mulching, and generally sound organic methods, but they mainly gave credit to the "divas" inside each plant. They communicated with the spirit of each type of plant, watching and listening as the plants somehow let them know what was needed, whether they needed more or less water or a different location. It was wildly strange and interesting!

According to the books (there were two books, I believe, but I'm not sure, and don't even remember the titles!) the wonder of these Findhorn gardens spread across the U.K., and people began to visit, just to see the incredible, lush, highly productive gardens. Botanists and horticulturists came and took pictures of the wonder vegetables: cabbage heads as big as washtubs, English peas that produced a bushel of peas per plant. Unheard of, unbelievable results from an area so harsh and forbidding. Poor soil, raging salt-laden gales, and freezing temperatures.

Some of the scientists figured that the explanation for these wonder-gardens was not soil or weather or gardening practices, but rather the astrological placement of the gardens upon the planet, sort of Stonehenge or Chaco Canyon, only affecting growth of vegetation. Astro-physical, quantum physical something-or-other. No one really knew why the Findhorn gardens produced the myriad of spectacular vegetables and herbs and flowers, only that it seemed mystical. Even magic.

Well I just loved the Findhorn story, and I began really looking at my herbs and flowers in the back yard flowerbed and trying to listen to them. I never saw one of the Findhorn divas that inhabited each plant, but I did get to know them really well. The results were heart-warming. My flowerbeds in the back yard were truly fine, I think, but they were for flowers and herbs only.

After several years of reading and planting in our back yard, as well as sort of trailing along with Papa in his giant vegetable garden, I asked Bert one day if I might have my own vegetable garden. Since there was plenty of land around, and lots of equipment, he said sure, why not?

There was a small area I had been watching adjacent to Papa's big garden. This spot was bordered by the lane on the north side and a worn path on the south, separating my garden from Papa's. The other two sides were marked by

(1) a huge old row of horseradish which had been growing there for years, and which no one ever dug or used, and (2) the big metal building which housed the tractors, hay-baler, corn pickers, and other farm equipment.

I showed Bert where I wanted my garden, and he plowed up and tilled it for me, then left me alone to do what I would with it.

I sat down one day and drew a little picture of the way I wanted to plant: not in rows, but in small patches.

Then I began hauling fertilizer. Hank had raised quail when he was in high school, and the quail house (really a shed) was full of sawdust laden with aged quail droppings. Very, very rich and well rotted. I hauled one bucketful after another to the garden.

At that time I was teaching at the county high school, so my hauling time was limited to after school and weekends. It was very early spring, too early to plant, but warm enough to work the ground.

No telling how many bucketsful I hauled. Once or twice Bert saw me carrying buckets and came out with a wheelbarrow, which helped dramatically. Finally I had covered the garden with about 3 inches of humus-laden quail manure.

Bert agreed to run the tiller over it all, and he did. The soil was loamy anyway, and the sawdust made it even easier to work.

When he finished tilling, I asked Papa if I could have some of the old hay from the barn, hay that he didn't plan to use. He said sure. There were several bales that had gotten wet and had rotted too much to use for feed. And also, the winter was over, almost time to start cutting hay again.

So I began to haul hay one bale at a time, broken into three or four slabs.

I covered the garden completely with about six inches of hay for mulch.

By the time the garden was ready, the feed store was getting in small bedding plants. So I was ready.

I separated the garden into small mini-gardens and began to plant, some seedlings, others in seeds.

I had patches of cabbage, tomatoes, okra, squash, crook neck and pattypan, spinach, several kinds of lettuce, potatoes, onions, garlic, soybeans, dill, radishes. I can't remember others, except for the yams.

One day I was telling Danny Dutton, a student, about my garden, and he asked why I hadn't planted any sweet potatoes. I said I'd never grown them, didn't even know where to get the plants. He said you could plant the ones from the grocery store, but sometimes they wouldn't grow because they had been heated in order to preserve them for grocery store sale. He said his mother kept yams year to year and had some slips she planted. He said he'd bring me a few, and he did.

I had to move a whole patch of broccoli in order to make room for the yams. Danny said they would really spread, and they did. Those yams made the most glorious ground cover! Beautiful. And they stayed pretty until the autumn, when everything else was slowing down. I'm not sure how many slips I had. I think it was about nine little tiny stems. I planted three to a hill and let them grow. They filled their plot completely and spilled over into the tomatoes, giving them shade underneath, resting on the mulch. I harvested about 7 or 8 bushels of yams that fall. I couldn't believe how much fun they were to dig! It was just like digging for and finding treasure!

The garden was a huge success. We didn't harvest the freakish enormous vegetables of Findhorn Scotland, but the harvest was prodigious. And beautiful. Weed-free. Bug-free. The plants seemed to shimmer and glow with life.

One day a friend came over to pick up something or other. She was a lady over-busy, and she was rushing and tense as a bowstring. I invited her in and we drank some iced tea full of mint, with a nasturtium floating in each glass. I had made some cookies and used rosemary to season them. It was a nice little tea party.

She sat there and seemed to breathe more easily than when she had rushed in.

After we finished, I asked her if she'd like to see my garden, my own little Findhorn. She said sure, and we walked down the hill, turned into the lane, and passed the big shed, coming suddenly upon my garden. It did seem to be shimmering and quivering with life.

My friend Gail stopped, put her hands over her heart, and breathed, "Oh my. I feel like I've just come into church."

I believe that was the nicest, most memorable comment I got from anyone who looked at that little garden.

While there was no overt competition between Papa and me, I know that we kept close watch on each other's gardens. While Papa planted huge, long rows of his vegetables, especially tomatoes and green beans, my garden was made up of very small single beds. I only planted about 24 or 25 bush bean plants, "Tenderette," my favorite green bean, and only 6 tomatoes plants. I imagine that Papa planted 40 or 50 tomatoes. The harvest difference was spectacular. Day after day Bert carried up to our house 5-gallon buckets of gorgeous, perfect tomatoes. The beans produced enough to feed us almost all summer, plus many packages frozen for the winter. Papa's tomatoes couldn't come close to amounts or quality.

We didn't compete, but the contrast was striking. And obvious. I had to work hard not to gloat.

Every evening about sundown, I went through the garden and sang to it. I ended each day with

> *Now the day is over*
> *Night is drawing nigh*
> *Shadows of the evening*
> *Steal across the sky*
> *Jesus give the weary*
> *Calm and sweet repose,*
> *With thy tenderest blessing*
> *May our eyelids close.*

I've thought of that vegetable garden many times throughout the years. I think of it as my own personal Findhorn: mystical, magical, productive, and one of the most favorite memories of my life.

ENGLISH GARDEN TRIP

My sister Betty and I planned a garden tour to England during 2000. We shopped for the perfect tour, decided on the best area to visit, and had a great many conversations anticipating our big larky adventure. We made our decisions and booked a fabulous garden tour for the end of June and first of July 2001.

About a week before Tour Day, Betty had an emergency health crisis resulting in surgery and had to cancel.

After a bit of hand-wringing, telephoning, and general hysteria over "what're we gonna do now," we came up with our solution. My oldest daughter Sue would get a quickie passport renewal, and we would go on with the tour. So that is what we did.

The tour turned out to be everything good that Betty and I had shopped for. A marvelous guide, all meals and hotels booked and wonderful. The amenities were impeccable:

And then there were the gardens.

Ah! England! The beautiful green isle.

I think we toured maybe eleven gardens in all. Big, formal ones as well as smaller, more cottage-like ones.

The big formal gardens were old, old, old. Some had been designed and planted centuries earlier. The shapes of the layouts were interesting and impressive, but they had fewer flowerbeds than some of the other, less aged gardens.

After two or three days, they somehow began to run together. Each one was absolutely spectacular: beds and beds of flower varieties of every kind. Lots were familiar to us, but many were completely unrecognizable to our Texas gardening eyes.

We attended the Hampstead Garden show, one of the two most prestigious and enormous garden show productions in the U.K. There were tents and tents of themed plants; one tent featured winter-blooming plants and they had piped in snow on the ground with crocus blossoms peeping through, though it was July and very warm outdoors. The tent featuring springtime plants was full of blooming daffodils, hyacinths, iris, tulips, all needing very cool weather.

Each tent was completely different, representing each season.

One of my favorite areas in the garden show featured floral arrangements. In this area, there were a number of different categories, some requiring all white or all the same color of floral material. One category featured all-dry material.

My favorite area featured "creative arrangements." Here, the arrangers were given an array of odd and unusual objects. They were required to use ten of the objects, along with certain flowers to create an arrangement. Some of the things they had to use were combs, brushes, shaving mug, plumber's friend, soup can, garden trowel, and lady's handbag lady's lace glove. I can't remember nearly all of them, but there were several dozen objects to choose from. They announced when the arrangements would be available for reviewing. The floral designers would work on them for one hour, and then they would open to the public.

We hung around long enough to see the arrangements and they were fantastic! I couldn't imagine how you could possibly put any of those things together with flowers and create something credible. But they did. Some were pretty, actually. Several were bizarre, like looking at abstract art. Some were whimsical and funny. Overall, it was a fun experience.

Our English garden tour was packed full of experiences new to us, and I am so grateful and happy that those nine days of my life included a little glimpse of English life and gardens of so many different types.

ROCKPORT SALT LAKE GARDEN

In 2006 we moved Rockport, to a house on Salt Lake. It was a completely different climate from either Kentucky or Findhorn. Lots of salt-laden wind, fire ants, sand grass burrs, but otherwise sandy, loamy, decent soil.

I read several books about Texas gardening, and in each one the section on "Gulf Coast Gardening" was disheartening. Several people wrote that it could be done, if-if-if! But the salt air and the freaky changes in temperature were negatives.

I met a man named Todd Cutting at church. He was a big member of the Master Gardener Association in Rockport, and we became plant-swap-talking friends during coffee time.

As the months went by, I spent some time at my dresser in the bathroom. It looked out on the water, and beside the backyard was a boat ramp. On the other side of the boat ramp, there was a sidewalk on two sides of a rectangle of weeds, bordered on the far side by a rickety fence separating us from our neighbor.

As I sat there each day, I began dreaming about making that little plot a flower garden as close as I could get to Nene's old flower garden back in Edna. One day at church fellowship/coffee time, I asked Todd Cuttings if he were making a flower garden from scratch, right on the waterfront, how would he do it?

After a moment's thought, he told me to do it this way:

Put Round-Up on the whole plot.

Wait two weeks, maybe 3, for everything to die.

Then go to the Transfer Station/City Dump and buy a big load of mulch: They shredded wood and palm branches into giant mountains of mulch out there and sold it for 5 dollars per truck full.

Cover the entire plot of land with at least seven inches of mulch. Ten inches would be better. Then wait a month and till it as much as possible.

Wait awhile, working the dead stuff out and separating the areas for planting, keeping mulch heavy, and adding more mulch if needed.

Then plant.

Well, I did what Todd said to do, with Bert's blessing and lots of help. The Round-Up killed all the weeds, and after it was all brown and dried up, Bert took his tiller and chopped the dead weeds into the soil.

We went out to the transfer station in Bert's truck and paid $5.00 for a load of mulch. When we got home with it, Bert backed the truck up to the garden spot and we began to shovel. After the truck was completely empty and we had put the mulch on the garden spot, oh! no! It was not nearly enough mulch. In fact, it looked like just the tiniest amount of mulch had been spread. Not 1/4 of the garden had any mulch. What to do? We figured it would take a whole lot of truck trips to mulch that garden as much as I wanted. It seemed like an impossible amount of work.

The next Sunday I told Todd the mulch situation and he suggested I call a friend of his, a lady with a dump truck. I did, and this lady (a Master Gardener friend of Todd's) agreed to take her dump truck to the transfer station and bring me a truck full of mulch. She figured it would hold about 7 yards, and if that wasn't enough, she'd go get another load. The whole thing, she'd do for $60.00. What a bargain!

She made two trips in her dump truck, dumped the mulch in front of the garden, and left us to spread it out. I almost swooned with delight at all that mulch! Never mind the work of spreading it.

Well, needless to say, the rest of the garden-making was pure pleasure. I planned it and bought a couple of shrubby plants, vitex and oleander, for key places, then made trip after trip to Johnson's Nursery in Ingleside, filling the garden with bedding plants.

I had started preparation for my little flower garden in late October with the killing of the weeds. By the time it was ready for plants, springtime had come and the bedding plants were available.

I planted old favorites and tried a few new things, at least new things to me. Everything grew and bloomed, and I thought the little flower garden was beautiful.

Bert made a little arbor at its entrance, with seats on the inside, and I planted several kinds of vines to cover it. It never was perfect, like you see in pictures or in the English formal gardens, but it still made a nice frame for the little flower garden.

We tried several types of stepping-stones throughout, like Nene's, but really never got that right either.

Still, it was a lovely little garden and the first year it was tidy and colorful and beautiful.

The week that I considered it pretty nearly finished, we invited some friends over for a blessing of the garden. Thom Elliot, our beloved pastor, came and said some perfect words; I think I have a copy somewhere. There were three couples, and Thom. We stood in the garden and he did the little ceremony. One of the couples had brought us a St. Francis statue, so we placed it by the mini-bird bath in the center of the garden, behind a small rosemary bush, covering the Saint's feet. After the blessing, we all trouped back into the house for lasagna, salad, and lots of wine. It was a really lovely, memorable evening.

The little garden was a pleasure and a delight that summer and on into the fall.

I decided during the blazing hot summer that I would not do the planned, organized bedding plant garden for the next year. Instead, I would broadcast wildflower seeds and see what happened. So I ordered 1/2 lb. of seeds from Wildflower Seed Farm in Fredericksburg, two different combinations of seeds.

I followed the directions and one day in October, when we had the forecast of rain, I went out and scattered the seeds. The wind was blowing a gale, so the seeds went everywhere. Some even landed in my mouth! I had previously cleaned out the spent summer blossoms and left some which looked like they might winter over.

Time passed and the flowers sprouted and grew. By late March we were seeing a few blossoms, and by mid-April that little garden was awash in wildflowers. There were more varieties than I could even imagine. Some flowers I couldn't identify and had to look up in a flower book.

The garden looked like it had been water colored, and when the wind blew, as it usually did, the pinks and blues, yellows and magentas and purples flowed together like an Impressionist painting.

One day some friends came over, and we all went to look at the garden. John Gay, one of the friends, stopped and stared at the garden. I was so pleased to hear him say, very quietly, "Monet."

The third year and the fourth year of the garden were not the planned, dramatic ones of the previous seasons. Some of the perennials came back; some of the invasive ones took over. I spent time in the garden and loved it, but it got away from me and went topsy-turvy in unchecked, wild greenery and blooms and growth.

One of those years the Queen Anne's lace went berserk out there and the entire garden was a sea foam of white lacy blossoms. Beautiful and wild.

The Salt Lake garden lived a normal life. It was born, grew, prospered, succeeded beyond measure, gave great pleasure to me and a number of others, and then slowly returned to Nature.

I'm really glad to have been part of that garden's life.

GIVERNY

What can I possibly say about our afternoon at Monet's incredible gardens at Giverny? Everywhere you looked, you saw still-life possibilities for masterpieces. The plantings were spectacular. The flowers and trees, the rocks and water and arbors all worked to produce the kind of spectacular garden that justifiably draws millions of people every year.

It had a sort of different effect on me than I had imagined.

I was somehow overwhelmed. There was so much. So many beds. So many areas of planned, well-maintained beauty. As we walked and walked, looked and looked, I began to feel dazed, some kind of overchoice feeling like I get when I go into a big fine store with entirely too many choices. Too many people. Too much, too much! I wanted to find a bench, sit down and look at the ground.

While we were in the gardens, we came across a small house with a tiny garden in front, and inside the house you could buy coffee and sweets. We sat at a table outside and drank coffee, enjoying the blaze of flowers in the minute flowerbed, with birds hopping in and out of them. Just a postage-stamp spot of beauty. This gave me as much pleasure as looking at the famous bridge with all its acres of water lilies, exotic and lush flowers and trees, which filled your eyes too full.

Giverny is a spectacular garden. I am so tickled that, after all these years of loving and learning about, and living with gardens, I did get to visit the summum bonum, the gold standard, the Holy Grail of all gardens.

Giverny!

I'm just as happy that my dad's vegetable patches, Granny Pumphrey's big old garden, Papa's half-acre, my Findhorn, Salt Lake, all of these plots of soil and green things growing have been part and parcel of my time on this earth. And that Giverny has a place among the other wonderful gardens of my life.